PRINCEWILL LAGANG

Dating God's Way: A Christian Perspective

First published by PRINCEWILL LAGANG 2023

Copyright © 2023 by Princewill Lagang

All rights reserved. No part of this publication may be reproduced, stored or transmitted in any form or by any means, electronic, mechanical, photocopying, recording, scanning, or otherwise without written permission from the publisher. It is illegal to copy this book, post it to a website, or distribute it by any other means without permission.

This novel is entirely a work of fiction. The names, characters and incidents portrayed in it are the work of the author's imagination. Any resemblance to actual persons, living or dead, events or localities is entirely coincidental.

Princewill Lagang asserts the moral right to be identified as the author of this work.

First edition

This book was professionally typeset on Reedsy.
Find out more at reedsy.com

Contents

1	The Foundation of Dating God's Way	1
2	Building a Strong Foundation of Faith	4
3	Love as the Guiding Light	7
4	Purity in Heart and Body	10
5	The Importance of Boundaries	13
6	The Power of Prayer in Dating	16
7	Navigating Challenges and Redefining Success	19
8	Commitment to God and Each Other	22
9	Preparing for Marriage	25
10	Celebrating God's Blessings	28
11	Conclusion - A Journey of Faith, Love, and Hope	31
12	Book Summary:	34

1

The Foundation of Dating God's Way

Title: "Dating God's Way: A Christian Perspective"

As Sarah sat down with her steaming cup of tea, the cozy warmth of her favorite reading chair welcomed her. She glanced at the title of the book she had just opened, "Dating God's Way: A Christian Perspective." It was the beginning of a journey into understanding the beauty and challenges of dating from a Christian standpoint. In this first chapter, we'll explore the foundational principles that underpin this perspective.

Introduction

In today's world, the concept of dating often seems like a complex, ever-evolving labyrinth with shifting norms, expectations, and values. With the advent of online dating, social media, and an increasing emphasis on individualism, the Christian perspective on dating provides a much-needed compass. It's a guide rooted in faith, love, and a deep understanding of God's plan for relationships.

Defining Dating God's Way

Before delving into the intricacies of Christian dating, it's essential to define what "dating God's way" truly means. It's not a rigid set of rules or an attempt to impose one-size-fits-all solutions onto complex human interactions. Instead, it's about aligning our dating lives with biblical principles, values, and God's will for our lives.

The Biblical Foundation

The Bible serves as the cornerstone of Christian dating. It provides invaluable insights into how to navigate the journey of romantic relationships with a focus on faith, love, and righteousness. Key passages such as 1 Corinthians 13, which describes love as patient, kind, and not self-seeking, are often cited as guiding principles.

The Purpose of Dating

Dating, from a Christian perspective, isn't just about finding a life partner. It's also an opportunity for personal growth, character development, and understanding oneself better. Dating God's way encourages a journey of self-discovery and building a foundation of shared faith and values.

The Counter-Cultural Approach

In a world where instant gratification often prevails, Christian dating may appear countercultural. It emphasizes delayed gratification, a focus on purity, and respect for boundaries. This counter-cultural approach is a testament to the deep-rooted belief that the best relationships are those built on a foundation of shared beliefs, mutual respect, and God's guidance.

The Role of Prayer

Prayer is a fundamental aspect of dating God's way. It's not just about asking God to bless a romantic endeavor but also seeking His guidance and wisdom in every step of the dating journey. It involves earnestly seeking His will for your life and being open to His guidance, even if it means making difficult decisions.

The Importance of Community

No Christian is an island, and dating God's way emphasizes the role of the Christian community in the dating process. Friends, family, and mentors play vital roles in providing guidance, accountability, and support during the ups and downs of dating.

Conclusion

As Sarah turned the page, she couldn't help but feel a sense of anticipation and clarity about what lay ahead in her journey of dating God's way. The foundational principles she had just read were like a roadmap for the adventure that was about to begin.

In the chapters that follow, we will explore each of these principles in greater detail and discover how they can be applied in the practical aspects of Christian dating. "Dating God's Way" is not just a set of rules; it's a way of approaching relationships with love, faith, and God at the center.

2

Building a Strong Foundation of Faith

Title: "Dating God's Way: A Christian Perspective"

As Sarah continued her journey through the book, "Dating God's Way: A Christian Perspective," she moved on to Chapter 2, eager to explore how to build a strong foundation of faith in the context of dating.

The Crucial Role of Faith

Faith is at the heart of Christian dating. It's the cornerstone on which a successful Christian relationship is built. In this chapter, we will delve deep into the significance of faith and how it affects every aspect of dating.

Understanding Faith

Faith isn't merely a religious concept; it's a fundamental element of trust and belief in something greater than ourselves. For Christians, it means placing their trust in God's wisdom, timing, and plan for their lives. In the context of dating, faith involves trusting God to guide your romantic endeavors.

Building Personal Faith

Before engaging in a dating relationship, it's crucial to cultivate a strong personal faith. This involves deepening your relationship with God through prayer, studying the Bible, and actively participating in your church community. The stronger your personal faith, the better equipped you are to navigate the complexities of dating.

Seeking God's Will

When it comes to Christian dating, it's essential to discern God's will for your life. This means prayerfully considering whether a person you're interested in aligns with God's plan for your future. Seeking God's will in dating often involves seeking wisdom and counsel from trusted mentors and seeking God's peace as confirmation.

Patience and Trust

Christian dating encourages patience in waiting for the right person and trusting God's timing. Rushing into a relationship or ignoring red flags can lead to heartache. Trusting in God's perfect plan may require waiting longer than you'd like, but it's worth it in the end.

Equally Yoked Relationships

The Bible teaches about the importance of being "equally yoked," which means sharing a similar faith and spiritual commitment with your partner. This principle ensures that faith is at the core of your relationship and minimizes potential conflicts in the future.

Accountability and Community

Accountability plays a vital role in building and maintaining faith in a dating relationship. Being part of a Christian community and involving trusted friends and mentors helps keep you grounded and provides valuable support and guidance.

Challenges and Testing

Building a strong foundation of faith doesn't mean a relationship will be without challenges. In fact, these challenges often test and strengthen your faith. It's during these times that your trust in God's plan and His guidance becomes even more critical.

Conclusion

As Sarah finished reading Chapter 2, she couldn't help but reflect on her own faith and how it had influenced her past relationships. She realized that building a strong foundation of faith was not just a recommendation but a necessity when it came to dating God's way. In the upcoming chapters, she looked forward to exploring more aspects of Christian dating, all rooted in faith, trust, and love.

3

Love as the Guiding Light

Title: "Dating God's Way: A Christian Perspective"

In her continued journey through "Dating God's Way: A Christian Perspective," Sarah moved on to Chapter 3, which explored the profound role of love as the guiding light in Christian dating.

Introduction

Love is at the heart of the Christian faith, and it should be at the center of any Christian dating relationship. This chapter will delve into the significance of love as it pertains to dating, emphasizing the principles of selflessness, kindness, and genuine care for one another.

Love Defined

Before we explore how love is applied in dating, it's important to understand what love truly means from a Christian perspective. Love, as described in the Bible, is selfless and sacrificial. It's not just a fleeting emotion but a conscious choice to put the well-being of others before oneself.

A Love That Bears All

Christian dating is characterized by a love that bears all things, endures all things, and never fails. This kind of love is resilient, and it extends grace and forgiveness to one another, acknowledging that we all make mistakes and have flaws.

The Role of Respect

Respect is a fundamental aspect of love. In a Christian dating relationship, respect involves valuing the other person as a unique creation of God and treating them with kindness and dignity. It means honoring their boundaries, feelings, and choices.

Healthy Communication

Effective communication is a manifestation of love in dating relationships. It involves active listening, empathy, and open dialogue. Christian dating encourages honest and transparent communication, which fosters trust and deepens the bond between partners.

Navigating Conflict with Love

Conflict is a natural part of any relationship, but how it's handled can make all the difference. Christian dating prioritizes resolving disagreements with love and respect, seeking reconciliation rather than winning arguments.

The Role of Intimacy

Physical intimacy has its place in a Christian dating relationship, but it must be approached with love and respect. Love guides couples to honor God's design for intimacy, which includes waiting until marriage for sexual intimacy, and valuing emotional and spiritual intimacy alongside physical closeness.

Boundaries as an Expression of Love

Setting boundaries is an act of love in Christian dating. Boundaries protect the sanctity of the relationship, ensure purity, and help couples maintain their commitment to God's principles. Love, in this context, means respecting and upholding these boundaries.

Conclusion

As Sarah finished reading Chapter 3, she felt a deeper understanding of the profound role of love in Christian dating. Love, as defined by Christian principles, isn't just a feeling; it's a way of life that guides every aspect of a relationship. With this understanding, she looked forward to the chapters ahead, where she would explore practical ways to incorporate love into her own dating journey.

4

Purity in Heart and Body

Title: "Dating God's Way: A Christian Perspective"

Sarah turned the page to Chapter 4 of "Dating God's Way: A Christian Perspective," curious to learn about the importance of purity, both in heart and body, in the context of Christian dating.

Introduction

Purity, in the Christian sense, encompasses not only physical but also emotional and spiritual aspects of one's being. In this chapter, we'll explore the significance of purity and how it plays a pivotal role in Christian dating.

Understanding Purity

Purity is not a concept rooted in judgment or repression but is a reflection of a commitment to living in a way that aligns with Christian values. It involves keeping one's heart, mind, and body focused on what is holy, honorable, and pleasing to God.

Emotional Purity

Emotional purity involves guarding your heart and your emotions, ensuring they are aligned with God's will. In Christian dating, it means avoiding emotional entanglements that compromise your commitment to God's plan.

Guarding Against Temptations

Temptations are a natural part of life, and they are particularly present in dating relationships. Purity calls for vigilance in guarding against temptations that could lead to impure thoughts or actions, such as lust or premarital sex.

Chastity and Sexual Purity

Christian dating places a strong emphasis on sexual purity. Chastity involves abstaining from sexual activities until marriage. This commitment is not about repression but about valuing the sanctity of marriage and following God's design for intimacy.

Honoring God in Your Body

The body is a temple, and Christian dating encourages respecting it as such. Honoring God in your body means making choices that preserve your physical health, which can include abstaining from drugs, alcohol, and risky behavior.

Accountability and Support

Maintaining purity in dating is not always easy. That's where accountability and support from trusted friends, mentors, and your Christian community come into play. They can provide guidance and encouragement when the journey becomes challenging.

Forgiveness and Second Chances

Purity doesn't mean perfection. It acknowledges that everyone makes mistakes. When impurity creeps into a dating relationship, Christian principles encourage seeking forgiveness from God and each other, and the opportunity for a fresh start.

Conclusion

As Sarah finished this chapter, she realized that purity was not about constriction or judgment but about fostering a deep and meaningful connection with God and with her future partner. It was a reminder that living a life of purity was a journey, and sometimes, it might involve setbacks. However, with God's grace and guidance, the path of purity was a noble and fulfilling one, a path worth pursuing in Christian dating.

5

The Importance of Boundaries

Title: "Dating God's Way: A Christian Perspective"

Sarah continued to explore the wisdom of Christian dating in "Dating God's Way: A Christian Perspective" as she turned to Chapter 5, which delved into the critical role of setting and respecting boundaries.

Introduction

Boundaries are like the guardrails along the path of Christian dating. They are not meant to restrict or confine but to provide guidance and protection. In this chapter, we will explore the importance of boundaries and how they contribute to healthy and God-honoring relationships.

The Role of Boundaries

Boundaries in Christian dating are like a roadmap for the journey. They help define what is acceptable and what is not, ensuring that a relationship remains focused on God's principles.

Defining Your Personal Boundaries

The first step in establishing boundaries is to identify your own values, beliefs, and limits. Knowing what you're comfortable with, what aligns with your faith, and what doesn't, is crucial for setting healthy boundaries.

Communicating Boundaries

Once you've defined your boundaries, it's important to communicate them clearly to your partner. Effective communication ensures both individuals are on the same page and respect each other's limits.

Physical Boundaries

Physical boundaries in Christian dating often involve decisions about how to navigate physical intimacy. It may include guidelines about kissing, holding hands, and reserving sexual activity for marriage. Respecting these boundaries demonstrates love and honor for each other and God's design for physical intimacy.

Emotional and Spiritual Boundaries

Emotional and spiritual boundaries involve guarding your heart and your spiritual connection. This might include being cautious about sharing deeply personal experiences, values, and beliefs. It also means maintaining a strong relationship with God individually while nurturing the connection as a couple.

The Role of Accountability

Accountability partners, mentors, or trusted friends play a significant role in maintaining boundaries. They offer guidance, encouragement, and support when the relationship faces challenges. Accountability keeps the relationship on track and aligned with God's plan.

Flexibility and Adjustments

As a relationship evolves, so can the boundaries. What was once comfortable may need to be adjusted over time. Being open to reevaluating boundaries ensures that the relationship remains respectful and in accordance with both partners' needs and spiritual growth.

Conclusion

Sarah closed the book after finishing Chapter 5, feeling a sense of empowerment in her Christian dating journey. She realized that boundaries were not walls that stifled a relationship but guardrails that kept it on a safe and righteous path. She looked forward to applying these principles in her own dating experiences and growing closer to God through the process.

6

The Power of Prayer in Dating

Title: "Dating God's Way: A Christian Perspective"

In the continuing exploration of "Dating God's Way: A Christian Perspective," Sarah turned to Chapter 6, eager to understand the pivotal role that prayer plays in the context of Christian dating.

Introduction

Prayer is a powerful tool that strengthens the foundation of Christian dating. In this chapter, we will delve into the significance of prayer and how it can guide, sustain, and bless your dating journey.

Prayer as Communication with God

Before discussing the role of prayer in dating, it's crucial to understand that prayer is more than a religious ritual. It's a form of communication with God, a direct line to seek His wisdom, guidance, and blessings.

Seeking God's Will

In Christian dating, the primary purpose of prayer is to seek God's will for your life and your relationship. It involves aligning your desires with His plan and inviting Him to be a part of your dating journey.

Praying for Wisdom

Dating often presents complex decisions. Praying for wisdom allows you to make choices that are in line with God's desires. It also helps you navigate the challenges and dilemmas that arise in dating.

Praying for Your Partner

Praying for your partner is an expression of love and care. It allows you to lift them up to God, seeking His guidance, protection, and blessings in their life. It fosters a deeper connection and mutual spiritual growth.

Praying for the Relationship

Praying for the relationship as a whole is essential. This means asking God to strengthen your bond, protect it from harm, and lead you both on a path that aligns with His will. It's a way of inviting God to be the foundation of your relationship.

Waiting on God

Patience is a significant component of prayer in Christian dating. Waiting on God means trusting His timing and His plan, even when you're eager for certain milestones in your relationship.

Praying Together

Praying together as a couple is a beautiful and intimate experience. It deepens your spiritual connection and reinforces the idea that God is at the center of your relationship. It can also be a source of strength during challenging times.

Community Prayer

In addition to personal and couple prayer, involving your Christian community in prayer can provide invaluable support and encouragement. Seeking the prayers of friends, family, and mentors helps you navigate the complexities of dating with added strength.

Conclusion

As Sarah finished reading Chapter 6, she felt inspired to embrace prayer as a fundamental aspect of her Christian dating journey. She realized that through prayer, she could draw closer to God, seek His guidance, and find the strength to overcome the challenges of dating while keeping her faith at the center. She eagerly anticipated incorporating these principles into her own dating experiences.

7

Navigating Challenges and Redefining Success

Title: "Dating God's Way: A Christian Perspective"

Sarah, eager to continue her journey in "Dating God's Way: A Christian Perspective," turned to Chapter 7, which delved into the complexities and challenges of Christian dating and how success can be redefined in the process.

Introduction

Christian dating, like any relationship, comes with its unique set of challenges and uncertainties. In this chapter, we explore how to navigate these challenges with faith and how success in Christian dating is not measured by conventional standards but by spiritual growth and alignment with God's will.

The Reality of Challenges

Dating, while a joyful experience, can also be filled with trials, doubts, and disappointments. It's essential to acknowledge the challenges and uncertainties that may arise and be prepared to address them with faith and prayer.

Redefining Success

In Christian dating, success is redefined. It's not solely about finding the "perfect" partner or achieving societal milestones. Instead, it's about growing in faith, developing strong character, and honoring God through the process.

Staying Grounded in Faith

Faith is the anchor that helps you navigate challenges. It provides the strength to persevere when times are tough, and it reminds you that God's plan is greater than any obstacles you may face.

Trusting God's Timing

One of the most significant challenges in dating is impatience. Trusting God's timing, even when it doesn't align with your own, is an act of faith. It means acknowledging that His plan is perfect, even if it doesn't match your timeline.

Embracing Rejection and Heartbreak

Rejection and heartbreak are inevitable in dating. Instead of viewing them as failures, they can be seen as opportunities for growth and self-discovery. These experiences teach resilience and trust in God's plan for your life.

Handling Differences in Faith

Differing levels of faith or faith backgrounds can be challenging in Christian dating. Open communication, mutual respect, and shared values become essential in navigating these differences.

Staying Accountable

Accountability, both personally and within your Christian community, is vital when facing challenges. Trusted mentors, friends, and family provide guidance, support, and prayer during difficult times.

Conclusion

As Sarah completed Chapter 7, she felt better equipped to handle the challenges of Christian dating with grace and faith. The realization that success in Christian dating was not solely dependent on specific outcomes but was deeply rooted in spiritual growth and alignment with God's will gave her a renewed sense of purpose and optimism in her own dating journey. She was ready to embrace the challenges that lay ahead, knowing that her faith would guide her through them.

8

Commitment to God and Each Other

Title: "Dating God's Way: A Christian Perspective"

As Sarah eagerly continued her exploration of "Dating God's Way: A Christian Perspective," she turned to Chapter 8, which focused on the significance of commitment in Christian dating.

Introduction

Commitment is a foundational pillar of Christian dating. In this chapter, we will delve into the importance of commitment to God, to your partner, and to the principles of faith that guide your relationship.

Commitment to God

The journey of Christian dating begins with a profound commitment to God. It involves recognizing His authority in your life, seeking His guidance, and aligning your relationship with His will. Your commitment to God becomes the guiding force in your dating journey.

Commitment to Self

COMMITMENT TO GOD AND EACH OTHER

Before you can commit to someone else, it's essential to have a healthy sense of self-commitment. This involves understanding your worth as a child of God, valuing your own boundaries and beliefs, and ensuring that you are ready to enter a committed relationship.

Mutual Commitment

In Christian dating, commitment to your partner is a promise to stand by their side, through joys and trials. It means prioritizing their well-being, respecting their boundaries, and nurturing a loving, Christ-centered relationship.

Pursuing a God-Honoring Relationship

A commitment to God and your partner means seeking a relationship that honors Him in all aspects. It involves avoiding actions or choices that compromise your faith, and instead, consistently seeking His guidance and blessings.

Cultivating Trust

Commitment builds trust in a relationship. When both partners are committed to God and each other, it fosters an environment where trust can flourish. This trust is the foundation upon which a strong and enduring connection is built.

Overcoming Challenges with Commitment

Challenges will inevitably arise in any relationship. Christian dating encourages using your commitment to God and your partner as a source of strength to overcome difficulties and conflicts.

The Role of Covenant

In Christian dating, commitment often involves viewing the relationship as a covenant. A covenant is a solemn and binding agreement that reflects the commitment you and your partner have made to God and each other.

Accountability in Commitment

Accountability to trusted mentors and your Christian community can help maintain your commitment. They can provide guidance, encouragement, and support, ensuring that your commitment remains steadfast.

Conclusion

As Sarah concluded Chapter 8, she felt a profound sense of the importance of commitment in Christian dating. The commitment to God, to oneself, and to a partner was not merely a formality but a sacred pledge that formed the backbone of a loving, lasting relationship. She was inspired to nurture and strengthen these commitments in her own dating journey, knowing that they would lead her closer to God and a meaningful, fulfilling relationship.

9

Preparing for Marriage

Title: "Dating God's Way: A Christian Perspective"

Sarah was nearing the end of her journey through "Dating God's Way: A Christian Perspective" as she turned to Chapter 9. This chapter would delve into the crucial aspects of preparing for marriage within the context of Christian dating.

Introduction

Christian dating is often a path toward the ultimate commitment of marriage. In this chapter, we explore the preparations and considerations that must be made to ensure a strong and God-honoring marriage.

God at the Center

A marriage built on Christian principles is one where God is at the center. Before marriage, it's important to ensure that both partners are deeply committed to their faith and that they understand the significance of making God the foundation of their union.

Shared Values and Goals

A successful Christian marriage thrives when both partners share common values, goals, and a vision for their life together. This requires open communication and alignment of beliefs and expectations.

Premarital Counseling

Seeking premarital counseling from a trusted Christian counselor or pastor is highly recommended. It provides valuable guidance, explores potential challenges, and helps couples develop the skills needed for a successful marriage.

The Role of Purity

Maintaining purity and sexual abstinence until marriage is a significant component of Christian dating. This commitment should continue as you prepare for marriage, ensuring that you both honor God's design for intimacy.

Navigating Family and Community Expectations

Families and communities play a crucial role in Christian dating and marriage. It's important to navigate their expectations and seek their blessings while also maintaining a strong boundary to ensure that the decisions made align with God's will.

Financial Stewardship

Preparing for marriage includes responsible financial stewardship. Discussing financial goals, budgeting, and financial responsibilities is essential to avoid potential conflicts in the future.

Preparing Emotionally

Emotional preparedness is as important as spiritual preparedness. Both partners should be emotionally mature and capable of providing love, support, and understanding to one another.

Praying Together for Your Future

As a couple, praying together for your future, your marriage, and your continued commitment to God is a powerful way to deepen your spiritual connection and solidify your bond.

Conclusion

As Sarah reached the end of Chapter 9, she felt a sense of readiness and anticipation. Preparing for marriage within the context of Christian dating was a profound journey, one that involved deepening her faith, aligning her values, and nurturing a loving relationship with God at the center. With the guidance from this chapter, she looked forward to the future and the prospect of a marriage firmly rooted in Christian principles.

10

Celebrating God's Blessings

Title: "Dating God's Way: A Christian Perspective"

Sarah reached the final chapter of "Dating God's Way: A Christian Perspective." This chapter was dedicated to celebrating the blessings that Christian dating could bring into one's life.

Introduction

The journey of Christian dating is a testament to faith, love, and commitment to God. In this final chapter, we reflect on the blessings that come with dating God's way, reminding us of the beauty and fulfillment that can be found in aligning our romantic relationships with Christian principles.

A Deepened Faith

Christian dating is a journey that deepens your faith. It's an opportunity to trust in God's guidance, to seek His wisdom, and to grow spiritually as you navigate the complexities of relationships. This deepened faith is a precious blessing in itself.

Genuine Love and Companionship

When a relationship is built on love for God and for each other, it can be a source of genuine love and companionship. It's a bond that stands strong through the challenges of life and becomes a source of joy, strength, and comfort.

Spiritual Growth

Christian dating is a journey of growth, not just as individuals but as a couple. It encourages mutual spiritual development and a shared commitment to living out the Christian faith.

Fulfillment of God's Plan

There's a unique fulfillment in knowing that you are following God's plan for your life. Christian dating allows you to be a part of a story that God has beautifully crafted, and this realization is a profound blessing.

A Strong Foundation for Marriage

When dating is done according to Christian principles, it creates a strong foundation for a God-honoring marriage. The relationship is built on trust, love, and a commitment to serving God together.

Supportive Community

Christian dating often takes place within the context of a loving and supportive Christian community. This community provides encouragement, accountability, and the blessing of witnessing the growth and development of your relationship.

The Beauty of God's Timing

Christian dating teaches the value of waiting on God's timing. When you look back and see how God's plan unfolded, you recognize the beauty of His timing, even if it didn't align with your own expectations.

Gratitude and Joy

The journey of Christian dating is a cause for gratitude and joy. It's a celebration of God's blessings and a testimony to the beauty of relationships when God is at the center.

Conclusion

As Sarah finished the final chapter of "Dating God's Way: A Christian Perspective," she couldn't help but feel a profound sense of gratitude and joy. The blessings of Christian dating were not just about finding a partner but about aligning her life with God's plan. She knew that this journey was a lifelong one, and with God as her guide, it was a path she would walk with purpose, faith, and love.

11

Conclusion - A Journey of Faith, Love, and Hope

Title: "Dating God's Way: A Christian Perspective"

Sarah had reached the final chapter of "Dating God's Way: A Christian Perspective." In this concluding chapter, she reflected on her journey and the profound insights she had gained.

Introduction

The concluding chapter of "Dating God's Way: A Christian Perspective" serves as a moment of reflection, a time to recognize the wisdom and guidance offered throughout the book. It's a reminder of the importance of faith, love, and hope in Christian dating.

Embracing Faith

Christian dating is a journey that requires unwavering faith. It involves trusting in God's plan, seeking His guidance, and placing your faith in His wisdom, even when the path seems unclear.

The Power of Love

Love, as described in 1 Corinthians 13, is patient, kind, and selfless. It is the foundation of a God-honoring relationship. Love guides us in our actions, communication, and the choices we make in dating.

Navigating Challenges

Dating is not without challenges, but in Christian dating, these challenges can be seen as opportunities for growth, not insurmountable obstacles. Challenges can test our faith and our commitment to God's plan.

The Role of Prayer

Prayer is the lifeline of Christian dating. It is through prayer that we seek God's guidance, wisdom, and blessings. It's a reminder that we don't walk this path alone but with the Creator of the universe by our side.

The Beauty of Purity

Purity, whether in actions, thoughts, or intentions, is a cornerstone of Christian dating. It is a commitment to honor God's design for intimacy, preserving the sanctity of marriage.

The Importance of Boundaries

Boundaries ensure that your relationship remains focused on God's principles. They act as guardrails, guiding your journey and protecting the sanctity of your connection.

Preparing for Marriage

Preparing for marriage is an exciting and transformative part of Christian dating. It involves aligning your values, seeking premarital counseling, and ensuring that your commitment to God and each other is unwavering.

Celebrating God's Blessings

As you reflect on your Christian dating journey, you celebrate the blessings that come from aligning your love life with God's will. These blessings include a deepened faith, genuine love, spiritual growth, and a strong foundation for marriage.

Conclusion

As Sarah closed the book on "Dating God's Way: A Christian Perspective," she couldn't help but feel a sense of gratitude. This journey, guided by faith, love, and hope, had been a profound one. It was a reminder that God's plan was the most fulfilling and purposeful path in life. She was now ready to carry these principles forward, not just in her dating journey, but in every aspect of her life.

12

Book Summary:

Title: "Dating God's Way: A Christian Perspective"

"Dating God's Way: A Christian Perspective" is a thoughtful and insightful guide that explores the principles and practices of dating within the framework of Christian faith. This book takes readers on a journey that combines the sacred with the secular, offering a balanced approach to navigating the complexities of dating while staying true to Christian values.

Chapter 1: The Foundation of Dating God's Way
The book begins by establishing the foundational principles of dating from a Christian perspective. It defines "dating God's way" as aligning one's dating life with biblical principles, values, and God's divine plan.

Chapter 2: Building a Strong Foundation of Faith
The second chapter delves into the pivotal role of faith in Christian dating. It emphasizes the importance of a deep and personal relationship with God and how faith serves as a compass throughout the dating journey.

Chapter 3: Love as the Guiding Light
Chapter 3 underscores the centrality of love in Christian dating. It describes love as selfless, kind, and enduring and explores its significance in the context

BOOK SUMMARY:

of romantic relationships.

Chapter 4: Purity in Heart and Body

Purity, both in heart and body, is the focus of Chapter 4. This chapter explores the significance of emotional and physical purity in Christian dating and how it contributes to building strong and God-honoring relationships.

Chapter 5: The Importance of Boundaries

Chapter 5 delves into the critical role of setting and respecting boundaries in Christian dating. It discusses the importance of defining personal boundaries, communicating them, and how these boundaries contribute to a healthy and respectful relationship.

Chapter 6: The Power of Prayer in Dating

Prayer, as a vital component of Christian dating, is explored in Chapter 6. This chapter emphasizes the significance of seeking God's will, wisdom, and guidance through prayer in every aspect of the dating journey.

Chapter 7: Navigating Challenges and Redefining Success

Chapter 7 acknowledges the challenges and uncertainties inherent in dating and encourages readers to redefine success in Christian dating. It's a reminder that success is not just about the outcome but the spiritual growth achieved.

Chapter 8: Commitment to God and Each Other

The concept of commitment takes center stage in Chapter 8. This chapter emphasizes the importance of commitment to God, to oneself, and to a partner, discussing how it forms the foundation of a God-honoring relationship.

Chapter 9: Preparing for Marriage

Chapter 9 focuses on the preparations and considerations required for a strong and God-honoring marriage within the context of Christian dating. It covers topics like shared values, premarital counseling, financial stewardship, and emotional readiness.

Chapter 10: Celebrating God's Blessings

The final chapter, Chapter 10, reflects on the blessings that Christian dating can bring into one's life. It underscores the significance of faith, love, and hope in dating God's way.

"Dating God's Way: A Christian Perspective" is a comprehensive guide that offers valuable insights and practical advice for those seeking to pursue romantic relationships grounded in Christian faith. It emphasizes the importance of faith, love, purity, prayer, boundaries, and commitment, and serves as a roadmap for a fulfilling and God-honoring dating journey.

www.ingramcontent.com/pod-product-compliance
Lightning Source LLC
LaVergne TN
LVHW021055100526
838202LV00083B/5992